Grandma's Dead

Breaking Bad News
with Baby Animals

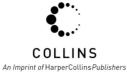

COLLINS
An Imprint of HarperCollins *Publishers*

Amanda McCall *and* **Ben Schwartz**

HarperCollins books may be purchased for educational, business, or sales promotional use. For information, please write: Special Markets Department, HarperCollins Publishers, 10 East 53rd Street, New York, NY 10022.

FIRST EDITION

ISBN 978-0-06-167376-4

08 09 10 11 12 ID/PC 10 9 8 7 6 5 4 3

Introduction

Afraid to tell your girlfriend her ass looks fat? Need to let your neighbors know you're a registered sex offender? Why not let a lovable baby bunny in a basket do it for you?

Grandma's Dead: Breaking Bad News with Baby Animals softens the blow of even the harshest news, saving you anxiety and time. In this day and age, who has the time to spend a long, tearful afternoon explaining to young Bobby that his daddy's never coming home? Especially when there are three happy puppies in a pumpkin patch eager to do it for you!

Even better, sending a baby animal postcard provides the recipient with a precious keepsake that can be cherished for years to come. This way, you'll never have to remind your wife that you cheated on her—she can treasure that memory on a postcard forever!

No matter how sensitive the subject or awkward the circumstance, *Grandma's Dead: Breaking Bad News with Baby Animals* provides an adorable solution to life's stickiest situations!

I'm banging your wife

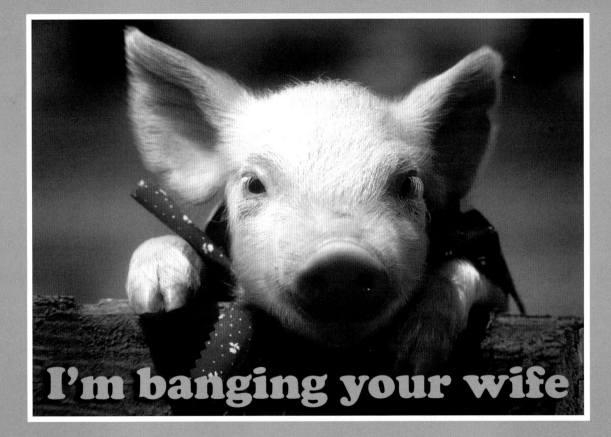

Grandma's Dead:
Breaking Bad News
with Baby Animals

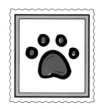

You don't matter

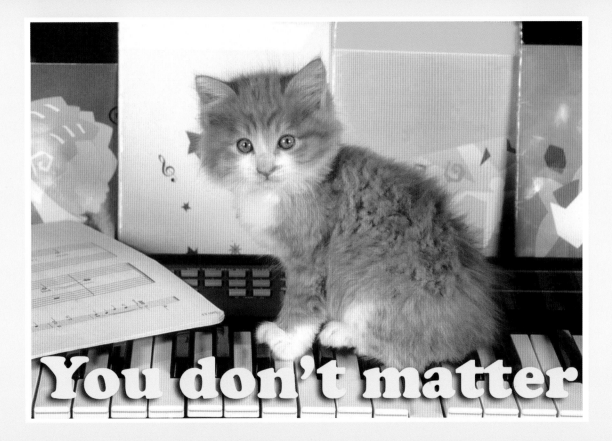

Grandma's Dead: Breaking Bad News with Baby Animals

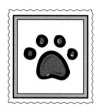

Mommy blew your
college fund on coke

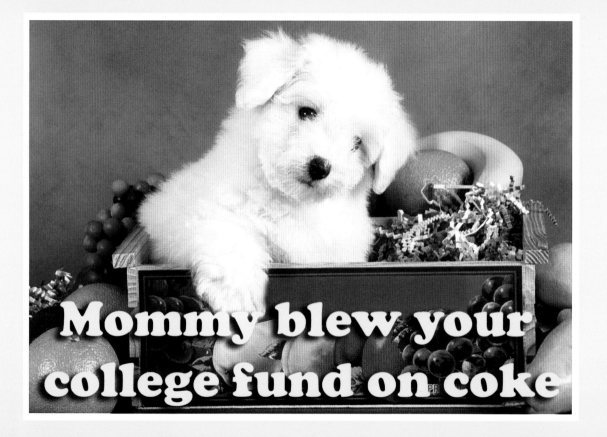

Grandma's Dead: Breaking Bad News with Baby Animals

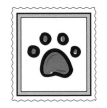

I used to be a man

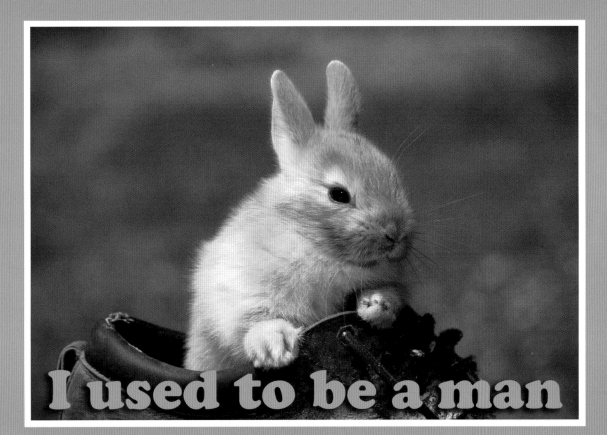

Grandma's Dead:
Breaking Bad News
with Baby Animals

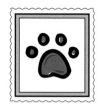

You're fired

Grandma's Dead: Breaking Bad News with Baby Animals

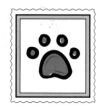

It's syphilis

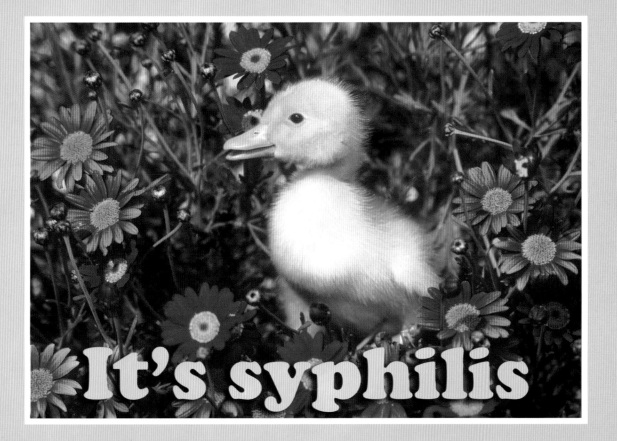

Grandma's Dead:
Breaking Bad News
with Baby Animals

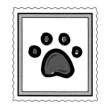

Daddy's never
coming home

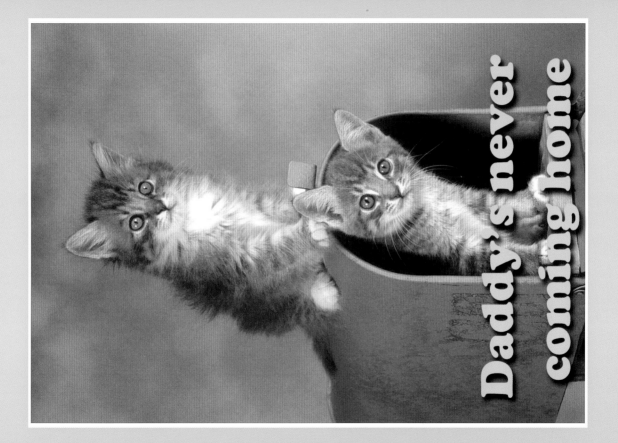

Grandma's Dead:
Breaking Bad News
with Baby Animals

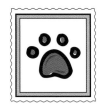

Your baby's ugly

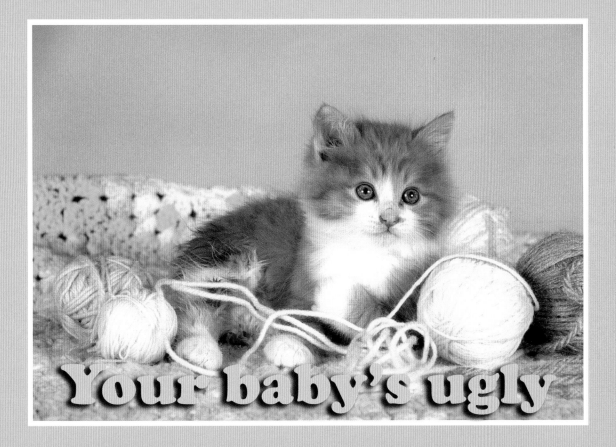

Grandma's Dead: Breaking Bad News with Baby Animals

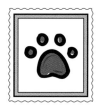

It's not me,
it's you

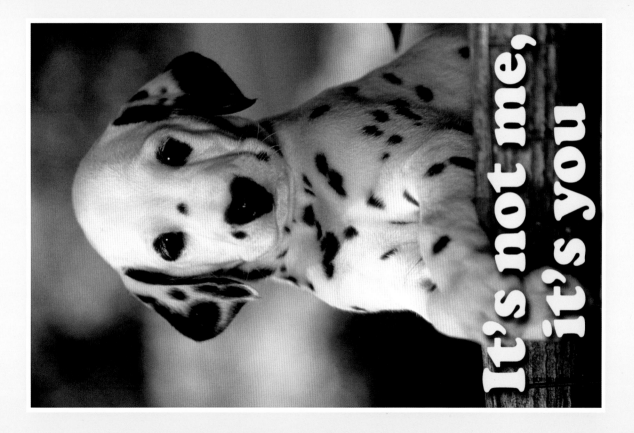

Grandma's Dead:
Breaking Bad News
with Baby Animals

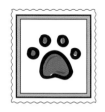

The donor backed out

Grandma's Dead:
Breaking Bad News
with Baby Animals

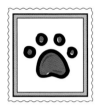

You're not invited

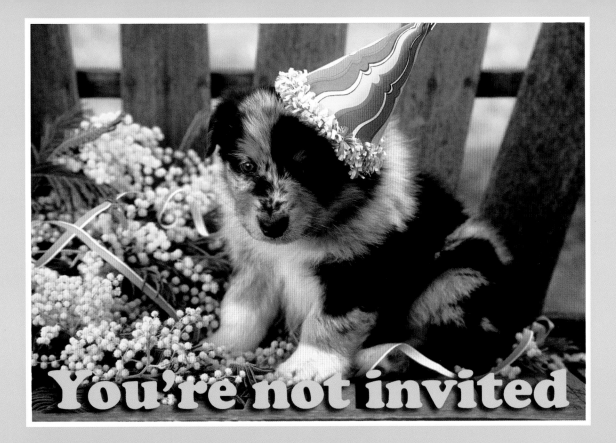

Grandma's Dead:
Breaking Bad News
with Baby Animals

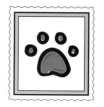

There is no Santa Claus

Grandma's Dead:
Breaking Bad News
with Baby Animals

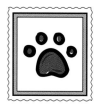

I
Y
u
You're my least favorite child

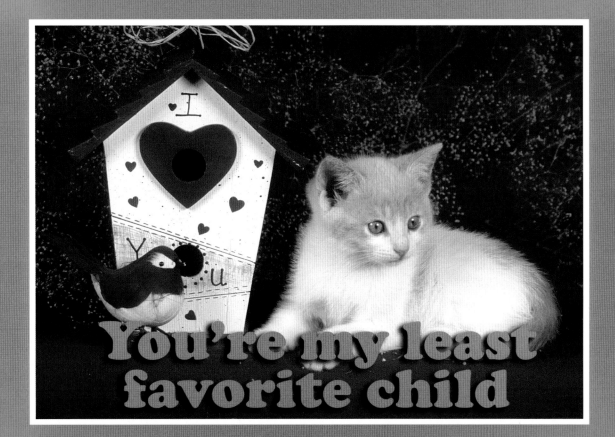

Grandma's Dead:
Breaking Bad News
with Baby Animals

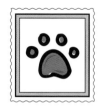

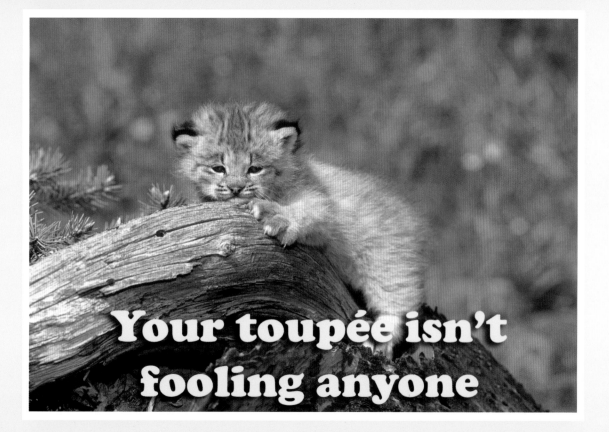

Your toupée isn't fooling anyone

Grandma's Dead:
Breaking Bad News
with Baby Animals

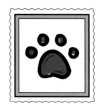

Sometimes I
pay for sex

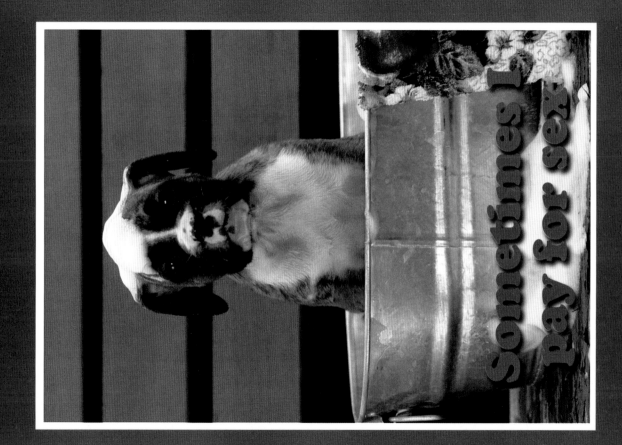

Grandma's Dead:
Breaking Bad News
with Baby Animals

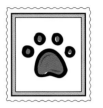

The meteor can't
be stopped

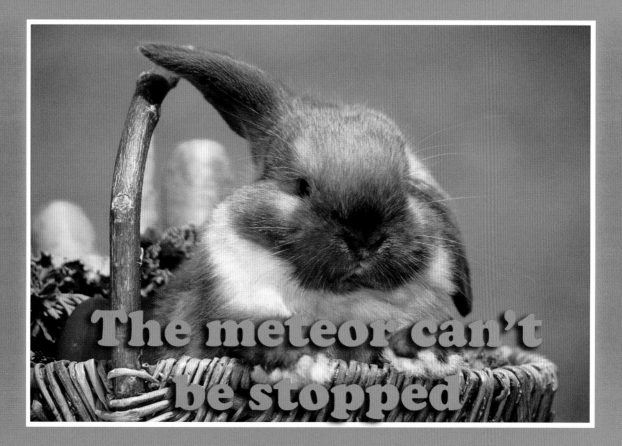

Grandma's Dead: Breaking Bad News with Baby Animals

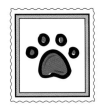

You'll never walk again

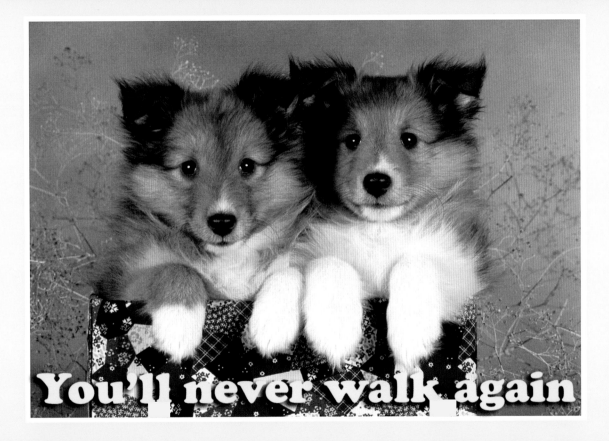

Grandma's Dead:
Breaking Bad News
with Baby Animals

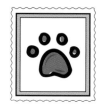

You're
the father

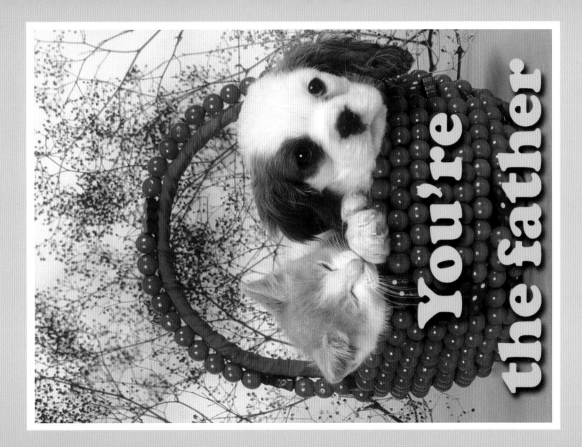

**Grandma's Dead:
Breaking Bad News
with Baby Animals**

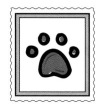

You're not the father

Grandma's Dead: Breaking Bad News with Baby Animals

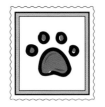

I'm a registered sex offender

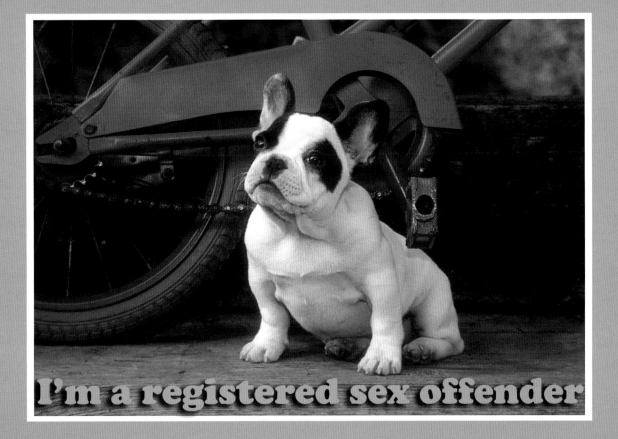

**Grandma's Dead:
Breaking Bad News
with Baby Animals**

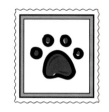

Dreams don't come true

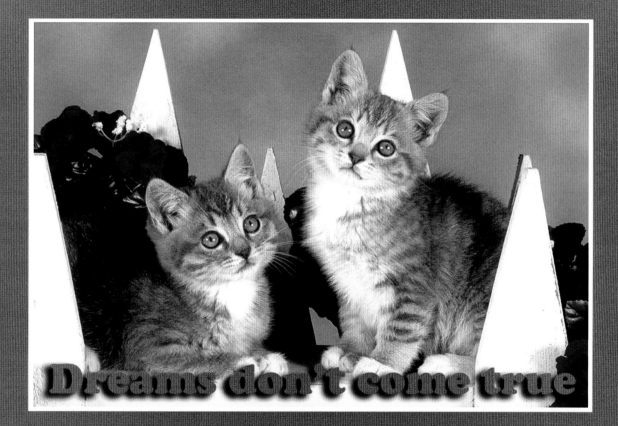

Grandma's Dead:
Breaking Bad News
with Baby Animals

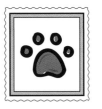

You're bad
in bed

Grandma's Dead:
Breaking Bad News
with Baby Animals

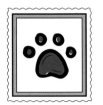

It's only sunny because there's
a hole in the ozone layer

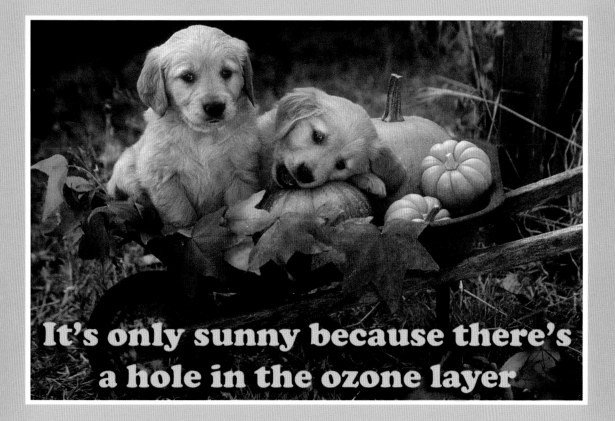

Grandma's Dead: Breaking Bad News with Baby Animals

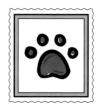

Your band sucks.

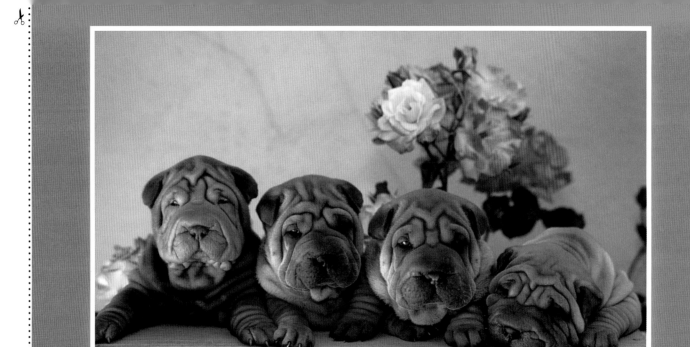

Grandma's Dead:
Breaking Bad News
with Baby Animals

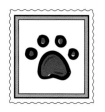

_____

_____

_____

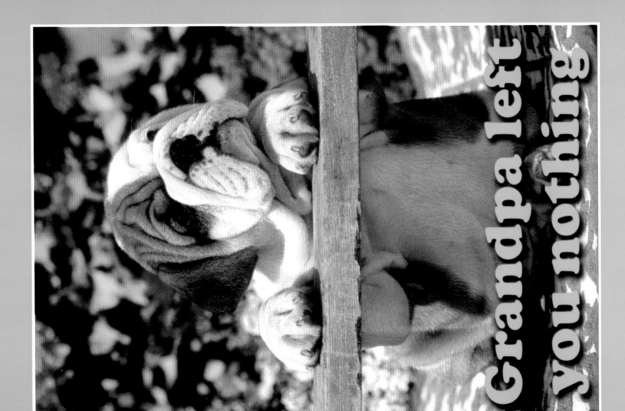

Grandpa left you nothing

Grandma's Dead:
Breaking Bad News
with Baby Animals

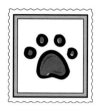

The condom broke

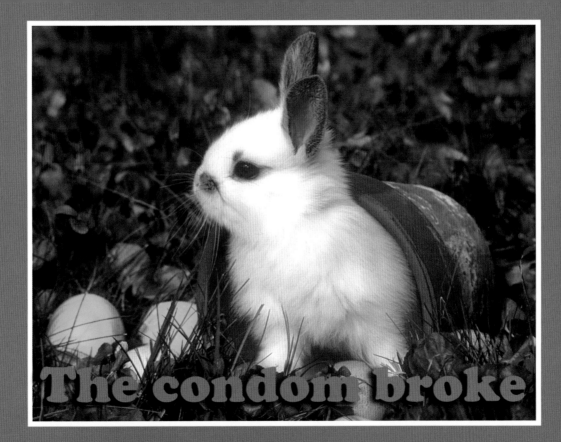

Grandma's Dead:
Breaking Bad News
with Baby Animals

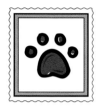

You're adopted

Grandma's Dead:
Breaking Bad News
with Baby Animals

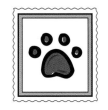

It's malignant

Grandma's Dead: Breaking Bad News with Baby Animals

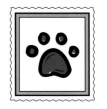

I married you
for your money

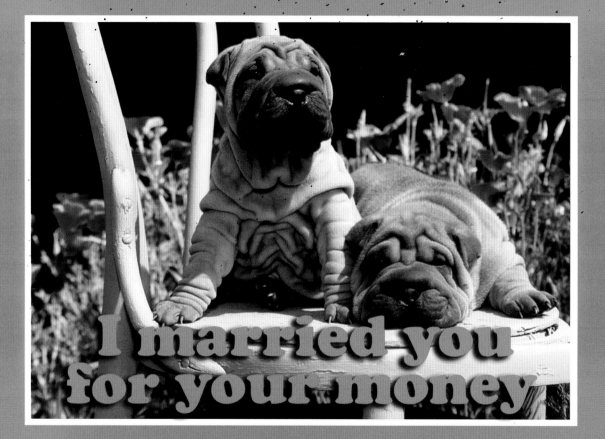

Grandma's Dead: Breaking Bad News with Baby Animals

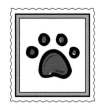

_____

_____

_____

Mom found your stash

Grandma's Dead:
Breaking Bad News
with Baby Animals

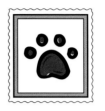

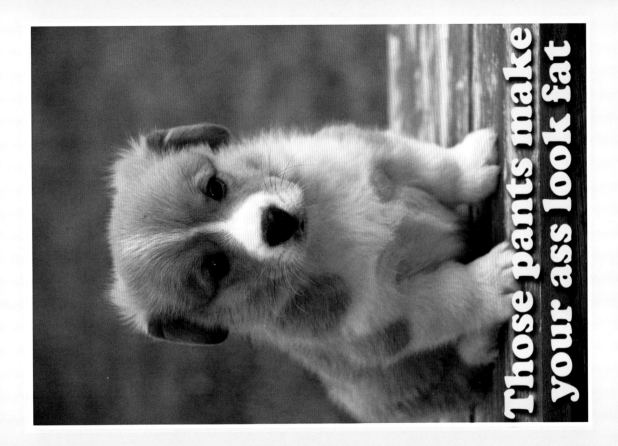

Those pants make your ass look fat

Grandma's Dead:
Breaking Bad News
with Baby Animals

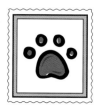

We have to amputate

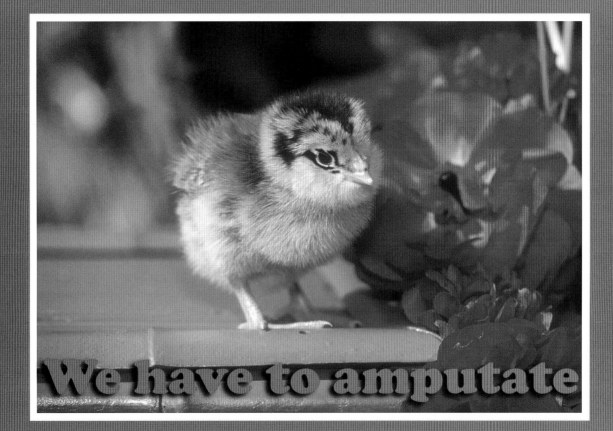

Grandma's Dead: Breaking Bad News with Baby Animals

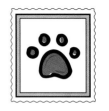

You have B.O.

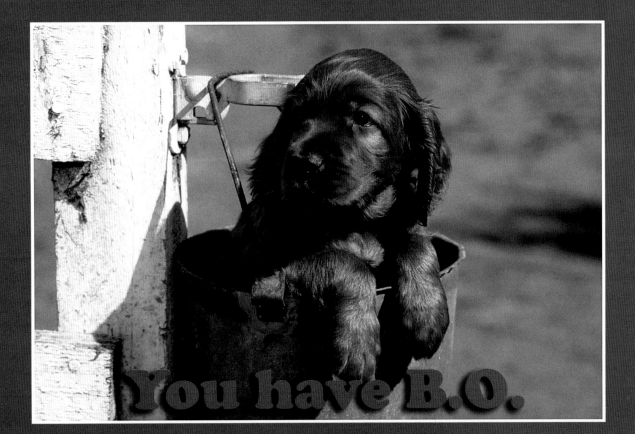

Grandma's Dead:
Breaking Bad News
with Baby Animals

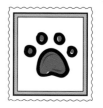

Recycling
won't help

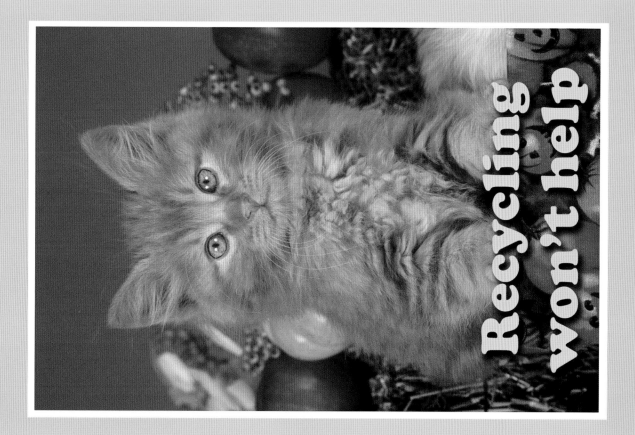

Grandma's Dead: Breaking Bad News with Baby Animals

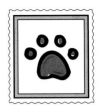

_____

_____

_____

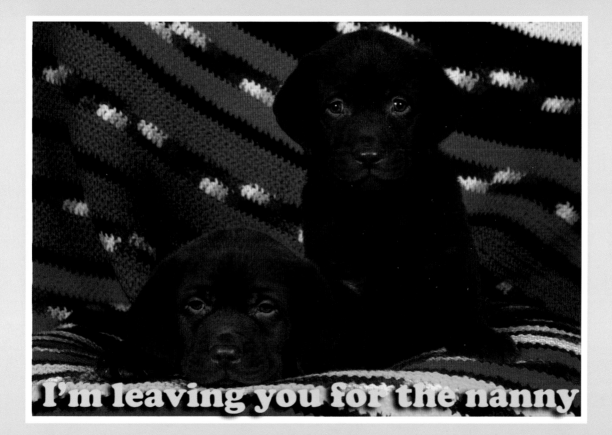

I'm leaving you for the nanny

Grandma's Dead:
Breaking Bad News
with Baby Animals

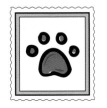

I'm saving myself for marriage

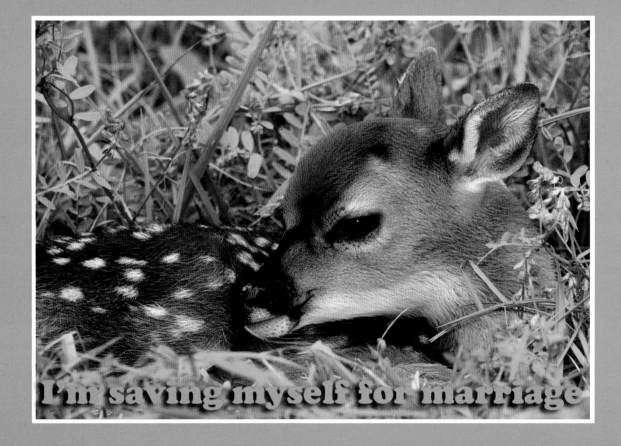

Grandma's Dead:
Breaking Bad News
with Baby Animals

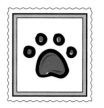

God isn't real

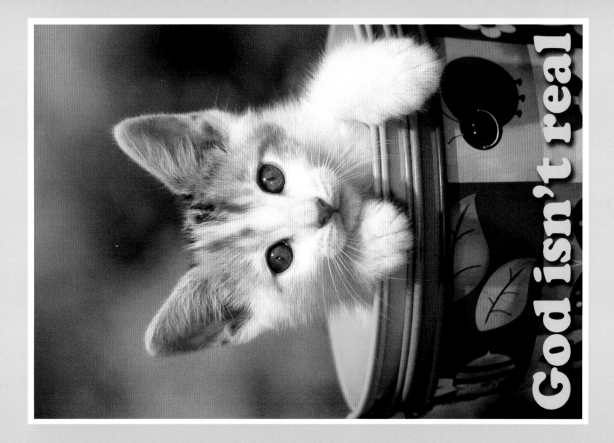

Grandma's Dead:
Breaking Bad News
with Baby Animals

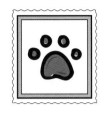

You were a mistake

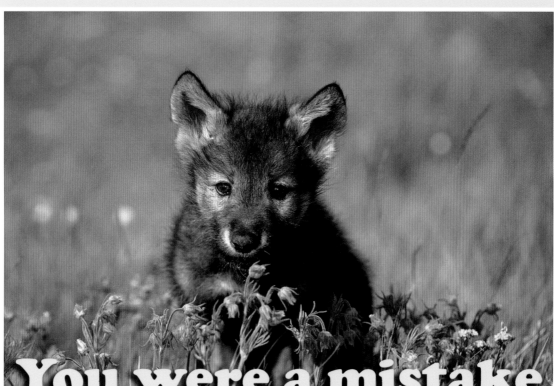

Grandma's Dead:
Breaking Bad News
with Baby Animals

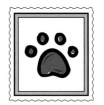

You're a terrible dancer

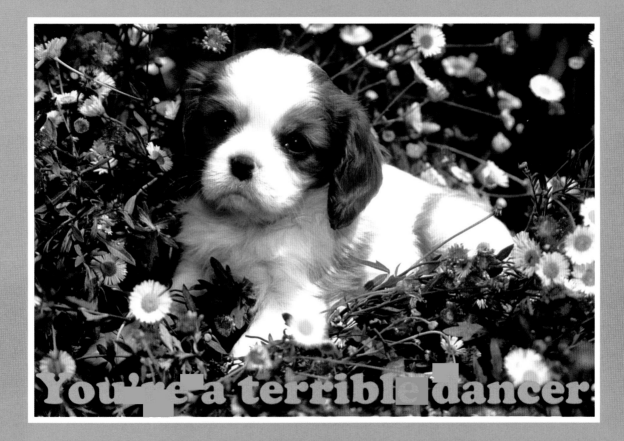

Grandma's Dead: Breaking Bad News with Baby Animals

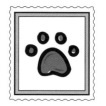

I'm into
weird shit

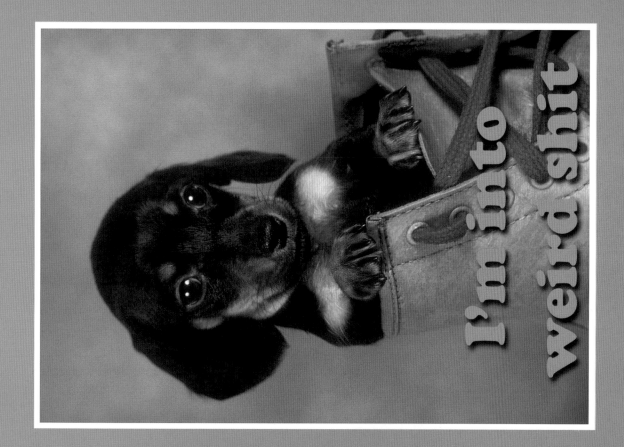

Grandma's Dead:
Breaking Bad News
with Baby Animals

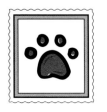

Acknowledgments

We would like to thank Jud Laghi, Rachel Miller, Jesse Hara, Stephanie Meyers, Bruce Nichols, Laura Dozier, Liz Kaye, Sharon Eide, Elizabeth Flynn, Tom Vezo, Adam Jones, Steve Dressler, and our loving families, who taught us everything we know about avoiding confrontation.

_____

Photo Credits

Lynx Kitten, White Tailed Deer, Wolf Pup © Tom Vezo
Lion Cub © Adam Jones
All other photos © Sharon Eide and Elizabeth Flynn/sandephoto.com